# Praise for *Forever Music*

"Pitch-perfect. It's really beautiful."
– CHRISTOPHER MERRILL, poet, essayist, director of the International Writing Program at the University of Iowa.


"Wonderful writing! I love every note Lera makes in what is really a tapestry of memories. It is permanently exquisite and impenetrable, this yearning and memory. Lera captures it so well – Russian childhood, its painful and exquisite beauty. This sense of beautiful, poetic urgency is in everything she writes. There is, in everything she creates a sense of genius in flight."
– THOMAS MCCARTHY, Irish poet


"Every single thing Lera Auerbach writes is astounding in its breadth and depth and brilliance. I know no one who can leap, spin, and surprise me as she can. The amount of space – intimate and world – she covers! I have no doubt that I am reading a genius of a natural, pure poet."
– EMILY FRAGOS, poet, anthologist.


"Anyone who deals with the psychology of creativity would discover here new unmapped depths. It is an unprecedented self-disclosure (…) In addition to a wide readership, it is of particular interest for scientists to explore the hidden aspects of creativity for psychologists, educators, and art historians. The fact that it is written in the voice of and from a child's perspective makes it an invaluable treasure."
– MIKHAIL KAZINIK, writer, musician, radio host, art historian

" ... Invaluable and fascinating guide for everyone who wants to introduce their child to the magical world of music."
– SOLOMON VOLKOV, writer, art historian

"Lera Auerbach is, in a word, a polymath of genius – one of the best minds at work internationally. She has led a fascinating life, and these poems tell part of her amazing story."
– JOHN MATTHIAS, poet, Editor at Large of *Notre Dame Review*

# FOREVER MUSIC

*Lera Auerbach*

DOS MADRES

2023

# DOS MADRES PRESS INC.

P.O. Box 294, Loveland, Ohio 45140

www.dosmadres.com    editor@dosmadres.com

Dos Madres is dedicated to the belief that the small press is essential to the vitality of contemporary literature as a carrier of the new voice, as well as the older, sometimes forgotten voices of the past. And in an ever more virtual world, to the creation of fine books pleasing to the eye and hand.

Dos Madres is named in honor of Vera Murphy and Libbie Hughes, the "Dos Madres" whose contributions have made this press possible.

Dos Madres Press, Inc. is an Ohio Not For Profit Corporation and a 501 (c) (3) qualified public charity. Contributions are tax deductible.

Executive Editor: Robert J. Murphy

Illustration & Book Design: Elizabeth H. Murphy
www.illusionstudios.net

Typeset in Adobe Garamond Pro & Cochin
ISBN 978-1-953252-84-5
Library of Congress Control Number: 2023940157

*First Edition*

## ACKNOWLEDGEMENTS

Many thanks to the Best American Poetry blog, where some of these poems first appeared.

Special thanks to Marilyn Nelson for inspiration and wisdom, to Emily Fragos, Thomas McCarthy, and Chris Merrill for shining the light in the labyrinth of my darkest hour, to David Lehman for his continued support, to John Matthias for his guidance, and to Robert Murphy for giving these poems a beautiful home at Dos Madres Press.

I am also eternally grateful to my parents, Lev and Larisa, for giving me the best childhood they could, to my husband Rafael for helping me to edit life, and to my two gargoyles – cat Aya and dog Finek who are the guardians of my solitude and (questionable) sanity.

*To my nanny, Marianna Shanyavska.*

# TABLE OF CONTENTS

About the Author

# FOREVER MUSIC

Lera Auerbach and Marianna, her nanny

*"Life can only be understood by looking backward;*
*but it must be lived looking forward."*
*— Soren Kierkegaard*

# (1)

Sounds, sounds all around.
I don't know words yet,
but I can feel the melodies of phrases.
Everything is music: the voices of people,
the wind outside, the bell of the streetcar.
When people speak loudly, I want to cry –
there are more sounds than I can hold!
I have no space left to breathe and gasp.
The voices become quieter, lower, slower …

I can breathe again.

*(Everything Is Music)*

(2)

A baby highchair is my throne for dining.
My subjects fasten me to the throne with buckles.
*(A monarch in exile.)*
I like my highchair – it offers perspectives.
I sit on my throne. In my hands, a red rattle
with wavy patterns – my royal scepter.
I shake it – and something rolls in its belly.
It clatters even louder when I throw it on the floor.
"A rattle is a person too – it may not withstand
such treatment – it may break," Mama tells me.
She sounds reproachful. I rattle the rattle.

How does a person break?

*(The Rattle)*

## (3)

Mama is teaching her students.
*(I am crawling on the rug.)*
I already know the notes –
Do-Re-Mi-Fa-Sol-La-Si.
Each note is a different color –
I imagine their incorporeal wings:
'Do' is white with a soft
rainbow overflowing on its feathers,
'Sol' is luminous yellow,
'La' is deep red.
I can see now:
sound is the flight,
and the trail of after-flight;
the wound left in the air,
disappearing traces of presence.

Sound is what continues to echo
in the memory when nothing is sounding.

*(What Is Sound?)*

(4)

"Look at your baby-stroller.
Look at it for the last time –
you will never see it again!"
Framed in the doorway,
stands my baby stroller,
red, taller than me.

But what is that 'never'?
What a strange word – so heavy –
this moment is engraved
in my memory: the red stroller,
the doorway, my mother's words.

*(What Is Never?)*

My parents do not buy a new stroller.
They roll me around in a folding carriage –
an accessory intended for a large doll.

I don't like that doll – *(I'm afraid of her)* –
her plastic complacency, her empty eyes.
*(But her carriage is helpful – I quickly tire of walking.)*

Better to fly while listening to music,
with incandescent creatures *(winged sounds)*
holding me up, not letting me fall.

*(Better to Fly)*

## (6)

My grandmother, Alichka, walks poorly.
Her legs are bowed like two letters C's.
Pain hides in each step. *(I can hear her pain.)*
Alichka brings me to Tsvilling Square.
*(She rolls me in the carriage from the doll I do not like.)*
On the bench sits an old woman with a mourning veil.
She is mourning for her son. There was a war.
Yura was ten. He was weak from hunger
and swollen from dropsy. He asked for a gun,
"Just shoot me, Mama!" The doctor said
Yura would not survive the night.
*(He did not survive.)*
Alichka asks, "Maybe you can help us
with Lera? Her parents are always at work;
she's too weak for a nursery, but it is
too difficult with my poor legs ... "
Marianna entered my life and my family –
the anchor and the lighthouse of my childhood.

*(Are You Still Watching Over Me?)*

## (7)

I'm three and a half. I can read words and notes.
I tell fairytales to my old Rönisch piano.
*(Without music, words lose their magic.)*

If I stand on one leg and press the pedal –
the wings of sounds become so long
they can fly far away into the unknown.

Yet I feel – I am still missing something.
All is distorted, not what it could be.
But what could it be? I don't know.

Where do the true sounds hide?

*(Searching)*

(8)

In every room,
I search for a hiding place:
behind a cupboard,
under a table.
I wish to disappear,
to find silence –
to hear voices
welling up from within.
There, in the darkness,
I gather sounds like flowers.

*(Cache of Childhood)*

(9)

Too bad I can't reach the piano pedals.
Mama does not let me play while standing –
she says it is bad for my professional education.
Mama is not home, and Marianna doesn't mind.
While standing, I can press the pedal and paint an ocean.
The ocean is calm. The ocean is enormous.
The ocean is the bluest of blues in E-flat major.
Arpeggios of waves slowly float under my fingers.
*Now a lonely sail appears amidst the blue mist of the sea ...*\*


The melody of the sail is full of awe. The sail is thirsty for the storm.
– Ah, you want a storm? I'll show you a storm!
*In between the sea and clouds proudly soars the stormy petrel.*
*He cries out and the clouds hear his joy in the bird's cry of*
*courage.*
*Thunder sounds in foamy anger, the waves groan with the*
*wind in conflict.* \*\*


A thunderstorm rages in C minor – lots of pedal, clusters,
glissandi of winds.
*The ocean was swollen and sullen. Its billows were boiling*
*with fury.*\*\*\*


The theme of the sail is still recognizable,
but it is disfigured by its daring dream.

It's drowning – the melody sounds lower,
sinking to the bottom of the unconcerned sea.
        The storm has passed. The ocean is calm again.
Triadic waves splash softly as if nothing had happened.
Only far in the clouds – a memory – the theme
of the dreamy sail. I sob with delight
at the drama that erupted beneath my fingers.

(*The Monstrous Power of Music*)

*Mikhail Lermontov, **Maxim Gorkyi, ***Alexander Pushkin*

## (10)

When Mama returns,
I want to play for her
the story of the brave,
lonely sail.
But music has changed –
I am unable to repeat it.
As in a crooked mirror –
what was beautiful
has turned into a caricature.
I'm crying,
no longer with delight,
but with sadness and shame.

Where did the true sounds disappear?

*(Where?)*

## (11)

"If you wish to save sounds, write them
as soon as they are born," Mama hands me
a *Notebook for Music.* I open it.
"But how to write them? With words?"
"Why words? You already know the notes.
When you have ideas for words – use letters,
but when you hear sounds – write notes.
"But *why* to write them?"
"With the help of notes,
you can return to the past;
with the help of notes, you can create the future.
Music notation is a time machine –
what is written – remains forever."

"Mama, what is 'forever?'"

*(What Remains?)*

## (12)

I wake up and remember – I must go to kindergarten.
I begin to cry. Papa comes to my crib.
*(I keep on wailing.)* Papa gives me a small jar,
"Here, take this – it's a piggy bank for tears.
Tears are precious – they should be protected.
If you are so intent on continuing to cry,
then cry into this jar – and save your tears."
I obediently cry into the jar, collecting tears.
Each drop – like a caught note in my *Notebook for Music.*
Perhaps music notes are unshed tears?

Where are you, my piggy bank of tears?

*(Unshed Tears)*

# (13)

My first day of kindergarten:
Marianna helps with my felt boots.
I climb out of my snowsuit – red mittens
on elastic bands are attached to the sleeves.
*(The empty snowsuit looks like an invisible man.)*

An older boy runs along the corridor,
and pushes me aside. I fly off into the corner.
I'm not crying. I am not allowed to cry
in front of strangers – Papa forbids it.
*(I cry only at home into the piggy bank for tears.)*

The room for the youngest group is at the end of the corridor.
*(The corridor is endless – as long as life itself.)*
I look back at Marianna, but she is already leaving
into the frosty day. *(I am alone here.)*

In the wardrobe hangs an invisible dead man.

*(Invisible)*

# (14)

In kindergarten, everything must be done *tutti*.
On command – children eat; on command – drink *kompot.*
You must finish everything on your plate!
I look at the gray *kotleta* (meat patty)
and the muddy *kompot* in my glass. A fly
is crawling on the *kotleta*. I imagine
how pleasant it is for the fly. I become
the fly. I lean closer, trying
to look the fly directly in the eyes.
The fly is in E major. The *kotleta* is in B minor.
My glass falls on the floor, the children laugh.
I am sent to the corner. *(I do not mind it.)*
In the corner, I can think about God;
about God, and the pieces of broken glass,
about the fly, and the spilled *kompot.*

In the corner I am free.

*(Don't Cry Over Spilled Kompot)*

## (15)

Kindergarten – frozen time –
a sickening temporal jelly.
*(A fermata on an unresolved cadence.)*

I am an alien stranded
on an incomprehensible planet.
*(The children are speaking in an unfamiliar dialect.)*

I cannot erase this maddening longing
for home. *(Why am I here?)*

Am I serving Time?
*(Did I deserve this sentence?)*

I am alone. *(Not alone enough –
someone's eyes are always following me.)*

Can Time be *served?*

*(Frozen Time)*

After lunch, we must sleep.
We are not allowed to be or to do –
it is *myortvyi chas* – "the dead hour."
The hour of murdered Time –
Time
sunk
into forever.
I close my eyes and see Time.
Time is bleeding seconds –
one by one,
one by one.

I count them.

*(Sunken)*

## (17)

Kindergarten is full of gleeful children.
*(I can't breathe from their shouting.)*
I find a red horse and whisper into its ear
the tale of a girl lost in Time.
If I digress from my story, the noise
will become unbearable. I also
secretly pray, "Dear God, if You exist,
please take me home, I don't wish to be here!
Please make it so that I will get sick
and will be allowed to stay home all day.

Dearest God, if You exist, take me away forever."

*(If You Exist)*

## (18)

God, in general, is an agreeable fellow.
He does hear my prayers – I often get ill.
When I am ill, I don't go to kindergarten –
I can stay home and read all day.
Adults love me more when I'm ill.
Their voices become more tender and quieter.
*(They finally have Time.)*

Where was their Time before I was ill?
Why did it return? Where did it hide?
Perhaps, in the Never where everything disappears?
*(Where is Never?)*

Will I never see my stroller again?
Will there never be a courageous white sail?
But I still remember my stroller.
And the sail – isn't it make-believe and not real?
Is music real?
What if I am only imagined?

Do I *really* exist?

*(Make-Believe and Serious)*

## (19)

God tends to get carried away. I can't read;
Mama changes the cold compress on my forehead.
*(It dries instantly from the fever.)*
Coughing tears me apart from within.

Sounds transform into stones – each sound
wounds my temples. The doctor says,
"I am so sorry, but she will not make it
to the hospital. Better say your goodbyes here."
The doctor leaves, Mama falls to the floor
in front of our bedroom door.

I fly around the room; I see Mama.
She is on the floor; she is crying and praying
*(even though she does not believe in God.)*
I see myself wheezing on the bed – but it is not me.

I am flying around the room. I am the sound –
infinite and free of sounding. I no longer
need a body. I am traces in the air –
I am the upbeat of the wing.

*(Winged)*

## (20)

Once Upon a Time, Death paid me a visit.
Death looked like Death is supposed to look –
a figure in a cloak with a void instead of a face.
A sickle in one hand and a hammer in the other.
    I recognized it because Mama played me
a song by Franz Schubert. In the song, a father
with a dying child rides through the darkness
on a horse, and the singer sings with different voices.
In the song, Death was frightening, but not so in life.
I was curious – what was waiting further away
in that Never, where everything disappears.
    I said to Death, "I know you – you came to Schubert!"
"I come to everyone," Death answered indifferently.
"Why do you not have a face?"
"I do; you just don't see it yet."
"Why do you need a sickle and a hammer?"
"What?!"
I pointed to the hands of Death.
"Ugh, that's nasty! You better answer that yourself.
I'm *your* death; I am how you have imagined me."
"So, you are not here; you are only in my imagination?"
"Nonsense! Who are you talking to, then?
Maybe *you* are the one who doesn't exist, not me?
Perhaps you are only in *my* imagination?"

We were silent for a moment.

"Death, are you he or she?"

"I am that, and the other, and the third one.
There are always three."

"Who is the third one?"

"The third is not given."

Death touched my forehead. Its hand was cool.

"Death, I wish to see your eyes."

"*Khochetsya, perekhochetsya, pereterpitsya* –
Wanting, wishy-washy wishing, keep on wanting,"

Death answered me in a high treble voice,
then added in basso profundo, "Knowing too much
will age you quickly, child." Then Death sang:

*"In Lukomorye, the ancient oak was cut.*
*The birch tree, too, axes brought down.*
*The scoundrel-cat escaped in plight.*
*Oh, where are you, my golden knight?*
*Come here, honey, let's share the night!"*

Death sang out of tune. I laughed.

"Well, there you are. Just three feet taller
than a chamber pot – and already a critic,"

Death sounded offended. "I have to go,
I have no time to sing songs for you."


"Goodbye, Death. Someday you will reveal your face."


*(Until We Meet Again)*

## (21)

God listens not only to me – but to Mama –
My body has become mine again.
Days go by, I am recovering.
One day, Papa takes apart my crib,
"You've grown; you can sleep in a bed like an adult."
I am delighted, but already on the first night,
I miss my old crib. It is no more.
The ocean called Never has devoured it – now
it's too late to ask for its return.
I walk around the flat, come to the clock –
and stop its pendulum.

I don't want to grow up.

*(Fermata)*

Mama is teaching at the music college.
Her students are grownups – young men and women.
I know them all. I imitate Mama's students
and play by ear, but most of all, I enjoy
improvising on the piano my own stories.

Mama instructs me to play scales.
Scales are dull. I make faces and laugh
at my reflections in the lid of the piano.
Mama is angry now. I don't like it when people
raise their voices. I run away and hide.

"I don't know what to do!" Mama complains.
"You are ruining her childhood," Marianna grumbles.
Papa says, "She needs sports, look how puny she is."
Marianna brings me from under the couch.
I'm too big, but she puts me on her lap.
"Over the bumps, bumpy bumps, into the deep pit –
bang!" At the word 'bang!' Marianna
throws me into the air. I laugh.

I laugh as if I were still just a baby.

*(Bangy Bumps)*

I watch how Papa helps Igor
to tie his red Pioneer tie.
"Iga, what does pioneegh' mean?"
*(The letter 'R' is not within my power.)*
"Nothing," Igor answers. He makes a funny face.
"How can something be nothing at all?"
Papa explains, "When you go to school,
you will become an *Oktyabryonok* first,
then a Pioneer, then a member of the *Komsomol.*"
"She doesn't have to join the *Komsomol;* it's not required,"
Igor interrupts him.
"And what happens then?"
"Then ... then you grow up and become a person,"
Papa sounds indecisive. Igor frowns
and snorts. His tie is still crooked.
"And who am I now?"
"You are a child."

"Isn't a child person?"

*("He Who Was Nothing Will Become...")*

## (24)

Marianna and I are at a summer retreat.
I am five years old. I have a wooden block-flute.
I blow melodies and imitate birds.

My parents left us – they have urgent matters.
What urgent matters could there be during the summer?
I play my flute. Igor is here.

He is a genius, a chess prodigy who has won
games against former world champions.
*(He is my brother, and he has very long legs.)*

When Igor walks, I must run after him.
I quickly get tired. Igor lifts me on his shoulders.
I am an eagle, a stormy petrel, a seagull.

Igor runs; I fly after him – I am the wind.
The wind plays the flute. Grownups lie.
I know – my grandma, Musenka, is dead.

*(I'm not supposed to know – I am a child.)*
That's why my parents left. I'll never see
Musenka again. Never. Ne-ver.

"Iga, do you know?" I ask, landing my flight.
"No," he answers seriously. Igor is a teenager –
almost an adult. Grownups lie.

*(He Knows)*

I play with a girl my age. Her name is Olya.

"Lera, who are you?"

"What do you mean? I am me."

"No, what is your nationality?"

"What about you?"

"I am Ukrainian," Olya speaks with pride,

reddening with pleasure. "And you are Russian, yes?"

"Yes, probably," I answer hesitantly.

I've never thought about this before.

At dinner, I ask, "Marianna, am I Russian?"

Igor stops chewing and places his fork on the table.

"Who told you what?" worries Marianna.

"Was someone bullying you?" asks Igor.

"No, Olya asked me."

"If someone asks, answer – I'm Russian."

Igor instructs me with a severe expression.

*(I am sensing something is false here.)*

"And if someone says something – tell me!" Igor's

blushing.

"What do you mean by someone saying something?"

"Nothing."

Igor is almost an adult. Almost.

Grownups lie.

*(Who am I?)*

Marianna boils water in a large metal kettle.
*(We use only boiled water for everything.)*
Mama reminds me, "Our water is dangerous.
Papa washed his hair with tap water once –
that's why he is bald." *(It is true –*
*Papa does have a bold round spot on his head.)*
"You won't lose your hair from just one wash,"
Papa says conciliatorily. I look at the water.
Mama explains, "You can't see microbes.
They are so tiny – they are invisible."
"You can't see radiation," Papa echoes. *
"It is just water. Stop frightening your child,"
Marianna says to them, combing my hair.
"Boil or don't boil – radiation stays."
Papa sighs. For some reason, he sounds defeated.

"Papa, what is radiation?"

*(Danger)*

* Chelyabinsk Oblast was the center of Soviet nuclear experiments.

For our daily walks, Marianna chooses the cemetery.
The cemetery is in a forest. We visit Marianna's grave.
*(Her future grave.)* The gravesite is fenced;
it has two marble slabs and two tombstones.
On one – a portrait of Marianna's late husband, Vanya,
in an oval frame with his birth and death dates.
On the other – Marianna's photograph from her youth:
a chiseled impregnable beauty; the year of her birth
and a space left for her future death.

"Greetings, Vanya," Marianna says quietly.
The grave is silent.
"Are you sure he's there?"
"He is there and also not there."
"What do you mean?"
"His body is there, but not his soul."
"Where is his soul?"
"With God."
"But why would God need his soul?
Doesn't God have his own soul?"
"Don't talk nonsense!"

"Maybe God *is* the soul?"

*(What Is a Soul?)*

## (28)

In the cemetery, I do not think of Death.
We clear the fallen leaves from the gravestones.
Then Marianna sits on a marble bench
and quilts a rug from strips of old rags.

I wander between the graves, collecting fallen leaves.
There are no people, only birds and trees.
The graves are all different: some are modest,
others have statues, marble slabs, pedestals.
Many artificial flowers… What for?

If the dead are with God, why do they need
flowers, statues, stones, monuments?
Why does God need so many souls?
How can He take care of them all?
*(He still must watch over the living, doesn't He?)*

Or maybe all souls in death merge together
into one soul – like rivers into the sea?
What if this sea *is* our God?

If God is the sea, why does he send a storm
that sinks my courageous white sailboat?
But there was never a real sailboat –

I invented it, or rather, Lermontov did
*(but it's one and the same.)* I also imagined
the sea – there *is* no sea.
If I invented it all, does it mean
God and I are one and the same?

I look around. I no longer see
Marianna and her future grave.
Which way to run? I dart between the statues.
"Lera!" From the distance, I hear Marianna.

I run towards the voice.

*(God and the Sea)*

# (29)

Papa brings a white-ish-gray creature.
"Let me introduce you:
Lera, this is Kos. Kos, this is Lera."
Papa says ceremoniously and gives me the kitten.
Kos, in response, releases his claws –
parallel scratches appear on my arm.
"Why did he scratch me, Papa, why?"
"He's just a kitten."
But I know better –
Kos has vowed to be my foe.

How can I make someone love me?

*(Declaration of War)*

Loving you shouldn't be so hard!
I'll sing you,
I'll play for you,
I'll play *with* you,
I'll scratch your ears —
*(if you allow it, of course.)*
I'll steal food for you,
I'll not tell on you,
I'll tell you my secrets.
You shall be my hero!
I'll defend you,
I'll dance around you,
I'll conduct your aria in my opera.
I'll search for you,
I'll call your name.
I'll climb a tree,
*(although you never asked to be rescued!)*
I'll clean your crime scene,
throw away the evidence.
I will run from you
*(but not* with *you.)*
I will take the blame,
Oh, loving you shouldn't be so hard!
My arms and legs display the art

of your bad temper. I keep running
towards the horizon, where your tail
beckons me from the other side of love.

*(The Other Side of Love)*

# (31)

Kos is looking at me without blinking.
His Siamese eyes are strikingly blue.
He is a handsome cat, intelligent, and angry.
He is now looking for someone to torture.
*(I know only too well who is that someone.)*

I look at Kos as I retreat slowly.
If I reach the living room, there is some hope –
I could slam the door in a sudden *sforzando*,
but the chances of such a lucky cadence are minimal.
*(Kos understands it just as well as I do.)*

He is in no hurry. His tail conducts my heartbeat.
His tail – the metronome. His tail – the pendulum.
*(How I wish I could stop all pendulums!)*
Sharp teeth and claws dig into my bare legs.
Marianna hears my scream and hurries to the rescue.

Kos, snorting contemptuously, leaves with his tail
raised tall like the victor's proud banner.
My legs reveal the maps of my defeats.

Can a silent metronome skip a beat?

*(A Tail's Tale)*

Papa takes me to figure skating school.
*(Putting on skates is a ritual.)* Papa ties the laces
very tight. I wear a woolen dress, tights, and a gray
hat with a visor and a large pompom.
"Well, how was it?" Papa asks after my first lesson.
*(I am covered in snow from head to toe.)*
"I do not know. We were taught how to fall.
For the entire hour: Fall – then get up.
Fall again. Fall, fall!"
"To learn how to fall," Papa says seriously,
taking off my skates, "is an art in itself.
Who knows, maybe it was your most important lesson.
If you learn how to fall – nothing can harm you.
If you learn how to fall – you can be fearless."

*(The Art of Falling)*

Mama takes me to meet Volgusnov.
*(He is one of the teachers at the music college.)*
His small apartment is filled with books:
books are on the floor, on the kitchen table,
the piano hides inside a cave made of books.
The host smells of dust, mothballs, and medicine.

"Play after me," he plays a melody.
"Can you make it into a march? How about a waltz?
Can you improvise a polka?"
"Did you know she has perfect pitch?" Volgusnov asks Mama.
Then turns to me, "Tell me, whom do you want to be?"
"I already am."
"Well, I mean, when you grow up – do you want to be a pilot,
or *(smiling suggestively)* a musician?"
"I want to draw and paint."
"Then draw this room."

He gives me a pencil and a piece of paper.
"I will tell you a secret. The secret of space."
He explains how to draw perspective.
I am delighted. My drawing came to life –
the horizon line beckons inland.

On the way home, Mama asks,

"Do you want to study with him?"

"Of course!"

"Then let's audition for the music school.

They are opening a special class for gifted children."

"Am I gifted?"

"You are you."

"Where are my gifts?"

At home, I search for the promised gifts,

but Mama just laughs.

*(Grownups lie.)*

Instead, I see perspective everywhere.

*(To find perspective, you need a horizon line.)*


The horizon is something that cannot be reached.


*(In Search of Horizon)*

## (34)

I am writing a song about fallen birds.
*(When birds fly – leaves fall. When birds fall – leaves fly.)*
A sad melody illustrates the lines.
I bring a fallen leaf from the cemetery to Volgusnov.
He places it inside a heavy Encyclopedia.
He corrects my rhythm, "Music is everywhere –
it's alive yet infinite – you are hearing it."

He smiles kindly, "Thanks for the leaf."

*(When Birds Fall)*

## (35)

Music is everywhere, but grownups do not hear it.
They're running around all the time, talking,
listening to the radio, watching TV, arguing, –
but it is all noise. I hide in the closet
and listen within. The sounds are calling.

"Pendulum, don't let me forget how to listen!"

*(The Call)*

## (36)

I am drawing a house. It's my Dream House.
Smoke rises from the chimney
*(my birthday cake is baking.)*
I have many friends; we hold hands together.
A meadow with flowers surrounds the house.
My drawing is beautiful. The next day,
I open my album: the rickety walls,
and violent smoke *(indication of fire?)*
The grinning teeth of my 'friends' are frightening,
the blobs of flowers – bloody splashes.
What happened to my perfect drawing?

How and when did I betray myself?

*(Betrayal)*

## (37)

My head is on the level of our kitchen table.
On the table – a large knife. Papa often sharpens it –
shink-shink – with a special stone. I'm alone.
I stand on my tiptoes and pick up the knife.
I am a knight with a magic sword;
a tragic knight – I have lost my beloved.
I turn the knife over, resting its blade
against my belly. Wouldn't it be better
to die on the sword than to live without love?
A voice in my head, "But if you fall on this knife,
you will *really* die." Forgetting the noble knight,
I reflect, "To fall or not to fall?"
If I fall, I will die – then I could see what happens
after death. But if I die, I will get in trouble
with Mama – she would be terribly angry.
I abolish the execution of a noble knight.

My old buddy – Time – flies to the horizon.

*(Abolition of an Execution)*

## (38)

Aunt Marina grows yogurt.
It lives in a special jar.
The yogurt is alive and hardworking –
*(it works on enriching culture.)*
Aunt Marina also has a son –
Maksimka – he takes care of the yogurt.
He says, yogurt likes Bach.
*(Maksimka can sense its desires.)*
Yogurt must have good taste!
In my dream, the yogurt balloons
to the size of a large cloud.
I am stuck in a jar with a closed lid.

I am suffocating from asthma.

*(Bach for Yogurt)*

## (39)

I am visiting Marianna's one-room flat.
The small hallway is separated by a burgundy
theatrical curtain with silky tassels.
It smells of dust and forgotten melodies.
In the chest in the hallway, Marianna keeps her treasure –
crocheted curtains, which she made in her youth.
"This is your dowry," Marianna explains.
"You will grow up, get married, and then one day
you will open the trunk, take these curtains out.
*(They will still be beautiful in twenty years.)*
Iron them first, then hang them on the windows.
They are waiting for you."
I nod.

*(Crocheted Future)*

"Why get married?" I ask Marianna.
"Yesterday, boys teased Maksimka and me
"the bride and the groom!" Now, he pretends
he doesn't even know me."
"Everyone gets married. That's how life is."
"I will be different – I will never get married!
What would I need a husband for?
We would only quarrel over what to watch on the TV."
"Well, I don't know. Everything might
come in handy – even a husband."
Marianna lovingly examines the petals
on her curtains, then sings. She sings in Polish.
The song crochets its yarn into minutes,
days, and years; it melts the air –
only the faint outline remains –
then fades.

In framed silence, I wait.

*(My Dowry)*

There are two armchairs in Marianna's room.
They are uncomfortable, with carved straight backs.
"In earlier times, people had great posture,"
*(Marianna straightens her back to demonstrate.)*
"Now people are too slouched for such chairs!"
The rest of her furniture is made of tin food cans.

Marianna survived two wars and famine –
she saved canned food for the rest of her life.
She made her table from hundreds of cans,
topped by a board with a long tablecloth.
Her bed is the same – just cans and a board.
She hides them under a burgundy quilt.
*(The scars are everywhere – under the surfaces,*
*behind the quilts, curtains, tablecloths.)*
The war is long over. Yet it is here;
in front of me, staring into my eyes.

I sit on the armchair. I feel its carved back
against my shoulder blades. *(Uncomfortable but safe.)*
I will not die, like Marianna's son, from hunger –
we are prepared for the future to come.
I sit straighter. With these cans and some luck,
perhaps, I have a chance.

*(Canned Future)*

## (42)

Chocolate candies – '*Mishka kosolapyi*' –
beckoning me from Marianna's vase.
Chocolates are rare, and these are my favorites!
Marianna notices my longing look,
"Take it, darling. It is here for you!"

I take the chocolate. The blue wrapper
shows three cubs and their bear-mom.
*(I am a bear-cub; Marianna is my bear-mom.*
*Bears like sweets – honey and candies.)*

I unwrap the chocolate, bring it to my mouth…
and throw it on the floor. The chocolate is stirring
all on its own – full of worms.

*(Wartime Chocolate)*

## (43)

Mama has excellent memory.
She develops her memory all the time.
I am required to develop mine –
every day I memorize a new poem.
Pushkin, Akhmatova, Pasternak, Tsvetayeva....
I must recite them "with expression."
"Expressing that on which she sat,"
Papa jokes. *(But it's not funny.)*
I am lazy – no more poems!
Mama becomes upset. Gravity
pulls her stronger – it is called
Hyper-10-Sion. It may kill her.
*(I am the one killing her.)*
I have no choice but to learn
one more poem; just one;
just a poem.
It's easy enough.
It's easy. Enough?
For her.

*(Memory Drills)*

# (44)

In the summer evenings, we gather –
Parents, Igor, and I – and read.
Books are chosen by Mama. My age
doesn't matter. For her – I am a small adult –
hence the reading of Tolstoy, Dostoevsky,
Bulgakov, O. Henry. I am enchanted
by a rare sense of peace and belonging.
Reading books unites us into one harmony.

Is that what family is?

*(Reading Out Loud)*

## (45)

Mama is a better storyteller than Shake Spear.
*(Her words are more interesting than his original.)*
"Mommy, you don't need to read books aloud –
just tell them to me in your own words."

*To Kill a Mockingbird* does not need retelling.
Every year we read Harper Lee again.
I am Scout. *(I don't like to wear dresses.)*
Igor is Jem. Papa is Atticus.
Siberia is Texas. We fight for justice.
Courage is when you know you will lose,
but still, you do what needs to be done.

When I grow up, I will, like Harper Lee,
write a book which will become a friend
to someone. I will share my stories
in notes and letters, colors and shapes.

Writing is the art of sharing.

*(Pendulum, Bon Voyage!)*

When our parents are not around,
Igor reads me books for children:
Brothers Grimm, Andersen, E. T. A. Hoffmann....
Igor is already missing his childhood
while steadily turning into a young adult.
His childhood is moving away from him;
mine is still at the beginning.
I hear the changes in his voice;
the threads connecting us are gradually breaking.
Igor is floating beyond the horizon.
I run after him – but I am far behind.
An Eternity apart.

*(Beyond the Horizon)*

Mama's system of nerves has lost its system.
She also has way too much pressure –
*Hyper-10-Sion.* Mama works a lot.
Her students are divided into bubbleheads and bloodsuckers.
*(Both types are sometimes combined in one person.)*

Mama often takes me to the music college,
where she teaches until midnight. *(I know –*
*Mama needs me there for her protection.)*
"Are bloodsuckers vampires?" I ask.
"Something like that."
"Don't you worry – I'm here and I will protect you."
The whole evening, I watch Mama's students to ensure
they don't bite her. I grow tired and lie on the floor
under the piano – a quick nap, and then
I'll be at my watch post again.

Mama wakes me. The last student just left.
We walk on the deserted streets of a cold city.
"Did the bloodsuckers drink your blood today?"
"What? Oh yes. They did. They always manage."

I snuffle sadly. I failed to protect her.

*(At the Watch Post)*

## (48)

I like it best when Igor babysits me –
he does not pay any attention.
*(Can attention be* paid?)
I get bored, "Iga, can we play?"
Igor is very serious, very big.
*(Ten years older – an eternity away.)*
"Iga, let's play."
"I have no time."
"Let's play a bit, just a little bit."
"Do you see this watch? The watch tells me –
no time to play."
"The watch cannot speak."
"Yes, it can. Listen. Don't you hear how
seconds move: tick-tock, tick-tock, tick-tock?"
"You don't need to obey them."
"I must."
"Iga, please…"
"Oh well, all right, if you manage to bite
this watch on my wrist, I'll play with you."
I try to bite; Igor twists his arm –
and I bite my hand. I am upset –
Time is my enemy.

Igor laughs.

*(Bites of Time)*

(49)

Sometimes the clocks release Igor –
we go for a walk to Pushkin Park;
or we decide to stay at home,
and Igor starts our old record player –
I conduct an orchestra, waving my arms.
I like Prokofiev – the fight scene between
*Montecchi* and *Capuleti* or the spice of Rimky-Korskov's
*Scheherazade* – I dream of exotic lands.
Ah, my imaginary orchestra is magical!

Igor reads Doyle to me; he turns off
the lights and lights a candle. In the darkness,
he howls like the Hound of the Baskervilles.
I know Igor is still my Igor,
but the candle flame is flickering, mirroring
the darkest tremolo within.

*(Almost Serious)*

Igor recites verses.
*(He thinks he is a great actor.)*
As always, he pays no attention to me.
I don't know the meaning, but the dramatic
delivery makes an impression.
Once, I repeated one of the poems
to my parents, standing like Igor in a pose,
copying his voice, intonations, and gestures.
Apparently, the verse was of a dubious nature.
The reaction of my parents was unexpected.
They laughed for a long time, wiping away tears.
Then they ordered me sternly to close my mouth
and never repeat this poem again.

Igor was reprimanded. It remained unclear why.

*(Poetic Torments)*

# (51)

Maksimka is bigger, but I am quicker.
I can easily knock him off his feet.
I win chess games one after one.
Maksimka, pouting, leaves the room.
*(All my attempts to reconcile are rejected.)*
Papa comes to take me home.
Maksimka blurts out, "Boys are better than girls,
and you can't change it!" I have nothing to answer.
"Papa, why did he say that?" I ask
on the way home.
"What happened?"
I explain.
"Well... next time, you could let him win.
Just to support his spirit. He is a boy."
"But it would be a lie!"
"It depends on how you look at it."
Papa smiles wisely.

Grownups lie.

*(Lies)*

## (52)

The division into boys and girls doesn't suit me.
Nobody asked me who I wanted to be!
I will not be a girl anymore, nor a boy –
I have decided – I am a dog!
*(If someone doesn't like it – it is* their *problem
and none of my doggy business.)* Woof!

I smile, bearing my milky canines.

*(A Dog's Life)*

Igor's teacher asks my mother,
"Are you concerned that Legh'a doesn't play with dolls?
Her mategh'nal instincts may be distgh'upted."
*(The professor, like me, can't pronounce the letter "R".)*
I snort, laughing. Mama shrugs.
"Child, what do you want to become when you gh'ow up?"
He looks at me as if I were a math problem that needs solving.
I blurt out the first words that come to my mind,
"An astronaut, a detective, an explorer, and a conductor!"
"And a mother?"
"Hmm?"
"Don't you wish to gh'aise children?"
I shrug vaguely. Professor triumphantly shakes his head.
He looks expressively at my mother.

Mama seems unsettled.

*(Undefined Theorem)*

Mama: "Lera, you should wear dresses more often."
Dresses are uncomfortable for:
– climbing trees,
– defending myself against evil Kos,
– climbing over the fence,
– playing soccer,
– riding a bike,
– rummaging through the sand,
– searching for treasures,
– fighting for truth,
– conducting an opera,
– hiding from everyone.
It's generally inconvenient to live in a dress.
"I am a dog, not a girl," I remind Mama.

Can a dog wear a dress?

*(Dressing the Dog)*

## (55)

I close my eyes and orient myself.
A dog can find its way in darkness –
out of the labyrinth of sounds.
*(To howl is best from within.)*

Dogs' tears are dark like snow
outside my window. Chelyabinsk is my kennel.
*(Chelyabinsk – the city of black snow.)*
What is beyond its invisible walls?

Someday I will break free.

*(The Kennel)*

# (56)

Mama is unwell. I don't understand it:
Mama does not cough; she has no fever.
What can I do to help?

Strange people come and take her to the hospital.
"She will return tomorrow, don't you worry!"
Marianna consoles me.

"No, she will not!" I run away and hide.
I look at the piano, noticing for the first time –
it has too many teeth.

*(Foreboding)*

# (57)

Alichka says, Mama will have a surgery –
the doctors will remove her right breast.
I do not see this as a significant loss.
"Why does one need breasts anyway?"
"For beauty," Alichka explains, "and to feed babies."
"But Mama is old. She will not have more children."
"Not old at all – she is just over forty."
"I don't see what's so beautiful about breasts.
Do all women have them?"
"All adult women, yes."
"They will grow on me too?"
"Yes, on you too."
"Can we do something, so they don't grow on me?"
"No way, you're a girl. But don't worry, it will not happen
any time soon." Alichka's hands
smell so delicious. I calm down and think –
I still have time to grow and grow;
And then we'll see what can grow out of me.

*(Growing Problems)*

Mama is in the hospital,
but I'm not allowed to visit.
I walk to the piano
*(my one-winged angel.)*
The silence is too loud –
I feel its internal crescendo.
I close my eyes and gropingly try
to tell my story. The piano responds
with an alarming chord.

It understands me.

*(Understanding)*

## (59)

Mama returns –
she is not herself.
*(Was she replaced?)*

I breathe in her smell –
her scent has changed.
*(I want my Mama back!)*

I stop the pendulum,
but I hear my heart
inside.

Can I un-break what is broken?
Can I rewind Time?

*(The Other)*

My aunt brings me an orange from Moscow.
*(There are no oranges in Chelyabinsk.)*
I place the orange on top of my piano.
*(The world is grey but here is my little miracle.)*
I decide to eat it after I have learned a new piece.
I practice while looking at the orange longingly –
it is right here, yet out of reach.

Maksimka is waiting for me to finish.
He says, "Pushkin loved oranges. He even
grew a long fingernail on his pinkie."
"What for?"
"As I said, to peel oranges!"
"Nonsense. Try to do it yourself."
"My nail is too short. You try."
"No, I am a pianist – I can't have long nails."

We share the orange – then eat the peels.

*(Pushkin's Pinkie)*

## (61)

Our TV is small and square.
A lot of things fit inside: cartoons,
news, the man with huge eyebrows
*(the younger brother of Marx-Lenin,)*
and a lot of hissing black and white waves.
*(Papa says these waves are "x-static.")*

Papa loves our TV very much.
Mama can't stand it, "Live your own lives,
not the lives of others. Think with *your* brains!"
Sometimes, I find it hard to understand her.
How can one think with other people's brains?
If I am thinking other people's thoughts,
then who is thinking mine?
"Stop this nonsense!" Mama sighs.

Whose thought is that?

*(Other Brains)*

Papa disobeys Mama and turns on the TV.
If it hisses and only shows the waves of static –
Papa, with a sigh, simply turns it off.
If the TV shows the eyebrows of our leader,
then all is all right too – *(Papa can't stand it.)*
But if there is hockey – we are in trouble.
"You are wasting time!" Mama raises her voice.
"Why?" I ask. *(Papa is quietly fuming.)*
"While you watch it, your own life passes."
"Life passes anyway," Papa argues.
"Yes, but when you are an observer, and not a participant –
you don't influence the outcome." The TV hisses angrily.
My parents stop talking to each other for a while.
They communicate through me. *(I am the messenger.)*
But what if I don't wish to participate in anything?

Can one influence by observing?

*(Wavy Particles)*

## (63)

Mama observes my piano lessons.
Afterwards, Mama explains to me,
"Here, your teacher is correct, but there
she is mistaken – play the opposite way!"
Do I listen to Mama or my teacher?
*(With whose brains should I be thinking today?)*
I bark. *(I am a dog.)* I remember my nose.
Sniffing, I search for the bones of truth.

I keep on digging.

(*Deciding What is Right*)

## (64)

Young pianists must learn some weird skills:
Kopecks are placed on top of my hand.
"Play scales, but the coins must not fall."
A book is placed on my head. "Now,
play arpeggios without moving your body."
"Raise your pinkie – the hand should not slump!"
I am bored. I don't see any point
in restricting my movements. I'd rather improvise.
I snap at Mama, "You are murdering music!"
She slaps my hands. The book falls,
kopeks roll and hide under the piano.
I don't pick them up – I look at my mother.
Maybe I am not hers? Can she return me?
Is there a return policy for unwanted children?

Mama commands, "Again!"

*(Unwanted)*

Long queues are everywhere. While we wait,
I play Bach's *Preludes and Fugues* in my head.
The queue is in an agitated state of suspicion,
*(yet it also seems suspended in space.)*

We hold our food-rations. We wait. *(Time passes.)*
I wonder if the rations for Time exist.
If so, how many have we wasted today?
The queue is polyphonic, like Bach's fugue.

Finally, Marianna buys a dead chicken.
In my head, Bach is dancing a happy gigue.
The dead chicken joins Bach in the dance.
*(He is gallantly holding its bluish wings.)*

Bach certainly knew how to play the queue!

*(Fugue on a Chicken Theme)*

# (66)

Mama says we are wasting Time.
She always looks at her watch, yet she never
finds her Time. She also complains
there are never enough rubles left
to take care of bills. Who are those bills?
Why does she need to take care of them?
I would prefer she would take care of herself!
When I grow up, I will give her a million
rubles – she can buy anything she wants!
But where will I find her Lost Time?
And how will I manage to give it to her?

*(Where Is Lost Time?)*

## (67)

Now I look at the clock more often.
Sometimes its hands are crawling; at other
times they fly, but for some reason, it is
the clock that is always right, and not me.

"How long did you practice today?" Mama asks.
"I don't know. Two hours?"
"You practiced ten minutes –
improvising stories does not count.
From now on, use the blitz chess clock:
when you stop playing – press the black button –
then you'll know how long you've *worked*."

"But you said it yourself: 'When you stop *playing*.…' "

*(Checkmate of Time)*

## (68)

There are different appearances of Time:

The large pendulum of the grandfather's clock.
*(I am not allowed to stop it!)*
In the kitchen, the old coo-coo clock lost its coo-coo.
*(Shhh… I freed the bird.)*

Then there is Igor's wristwatch that bites
*(when I ask for my brother's attention.)*
In the mornings, my nasty alarm clock screams.
*(Oh, please, just leave me alone!)*

There are numerous Time signatures in music,
*(Music is imprisoned inside the bars.)*
The metronome stands guard as a warden.
*(I attempt a prison break.)*

Time is verified in rhythms and notes –
*(composer's unshed tears.)*
The blitz chess clock now measures my practice.
*(Against whom am I playing?)*

*(A Blitz Game with Time)*

## (69)

Time has faces, intervals, hands,
digits, bones and ashes, memories,
lost teeth, leaves, crocheted curtains,
knives that are swords, wings of sounds,

preserved cans of food, ration coupons,
expiration dates, telephone numbers,
future graves, faded photographs,
chocolates with worms, captured notes.

Children know: Time does not exist.
We have only imagined its existence;
and now Time is imagining us.
*(We are creations of each other.)*

– Time, oh Time, be kind to me,
*(If You exist.)* Please be gentle and generous.
I promise, I'll take a good care of You.
I'll hold Your hand when You're lost in darkness.

I am here for You. *(Are You here for me?)*
It doesn't matter what is real.
I give You form. You give me – me.
I know – You have my own eyes.

*(What Is Real?)*

## (70)

We drive in our Lada. The window wipers
dance with raindrops – falling notes.
We are passing forests, full of murmur.
We are passing rivers. *(Can fishes sing?)*

I imagine a choir of fish with their mouths
opening – singing chorales to the moon.
In the backseat of the Lada, I open my *Notebook*
and write down the melodies the fish choir sings.

The notes are reflections of light, schools of fish,
droplets *(spilt from my piggy bank of tears.)*
The car ride is bumpy. I open the window –
the wind rushes in and plays with my hair.

We leave behind the city with its worries.
We leave behind arguments and fears.
Behind – illnesses, doubts, pendulums;
behind – scales, and the birds of death.

Ahead is the sky. The car grows wings.
We fly above the sea – I see my sailboat.
Fishes are dancing a gigue with Bach.
They are holding their fins. Bach is smiling.

Pushkin is waving at me from the sailboat.
He's peeling an orange with his long pinkie nail.
He gives the peels to his friend Lermontov.
*(They remind me of friends from my perfect drawing.)*

The car flies higher into the endless summer.
*(The sky is the bluest of blues in E-flat major.)*
The clouds are yogurts that escaped their glass jars.
*(They are full of culture they wish to share.)*

Next to the car flies a herd of winged horses.
I help them to navigate by conducting the clouds.
Ahead is our summer vacation – freedom.
Ahead is – forever – music.

*(Forever Music)*

# ABOUT THE AUTHOR

 LERA AUERBACH is a poet, writer, visual artist, composer, conductor, and concert pianist whose work has reached a global audience. She holds degrees from The Juilliard School in New York and the Hannover University for Music, Drama, and Media. Auerbach's first book in English, *Excess of Being* (Arch Street Press), explores the form of aphorisms. In 2021, she was awarded the Robert Creeley Memorial Poetry Prize. Auerbach's poetic style is characterized by its vivid imagery and emotional intensity. Her most recent book, *A is for Oboe*, written in collaboration with Marilyn Nelson, was published by Penguin Random House in 2022. The audiobook version of *A is for Oboe*, read by Thomas Quasthoff, received the AudioFile's Best Audiobook 2022 Award and was named an ALSC Notable Children's Recording for 2023.

Lera Auerbach is a librettist and composer, whose numerous works for opera, ballet, choir, and orchestra are regularly performed throughout the world. She has collaborated with the National Geographic Society on a multidisciplinary symphonic journey, *Arctica*. She has also collaborated with Yad Vashem – The World Holocaust Remembrance Center – in the creation of *Vessels of Light*, which received its American premiere at Carnegie Hall in April 2023. In addition to her education and degrees in the arts, Lera Auerbach completed training and certification in the field of psychology. She is currently enrolled in the Master Practitioner Program in Neurolinguistics, and studies Ericksonian therapy and hypnosis. Lera Auerbach was elected as a Young Global Leader of the World Economic Forum. She is a regular contributor to the Best American Poetry Blog where some of these poems first appeared.

Author photo by Grace Yu.

For the full Dos Madres Press catalog:
www.dosmadres.com